WORLD CLASS
CITIES
Moscow
Heather Kissock
AV2
www.av2books.com
I0796617

Step 1
Go to **www.av2books.com**

Step 2
Enter this unique code

DAIWQ1NLK

Step 3
Explore your interactive eBook!

AV2 is optimized for use on any device

Your interactive eBook comes with...

Contents
Browse a live contents page to easily navigate through resources

Audio
Listen to sections of the book read aloud

Videos
Watch informative video clips

Weblinks
Gain additional information for research

Try This!
Complete activities and hands-on experiments

Key Words
Study vocabulary, and complete a matching word activity

Quizzes
Test your knowledge

Slideshows
View images and captions

This title is part of our AV2 digital subscription

1-Year 3–8 Subscription
ISBN 978-1-7911-3306-1

Access hundreds of AV2 titles with our digital subscription.
Sign up for a FREE trial at **www.av2books.com/trial**

Moscow

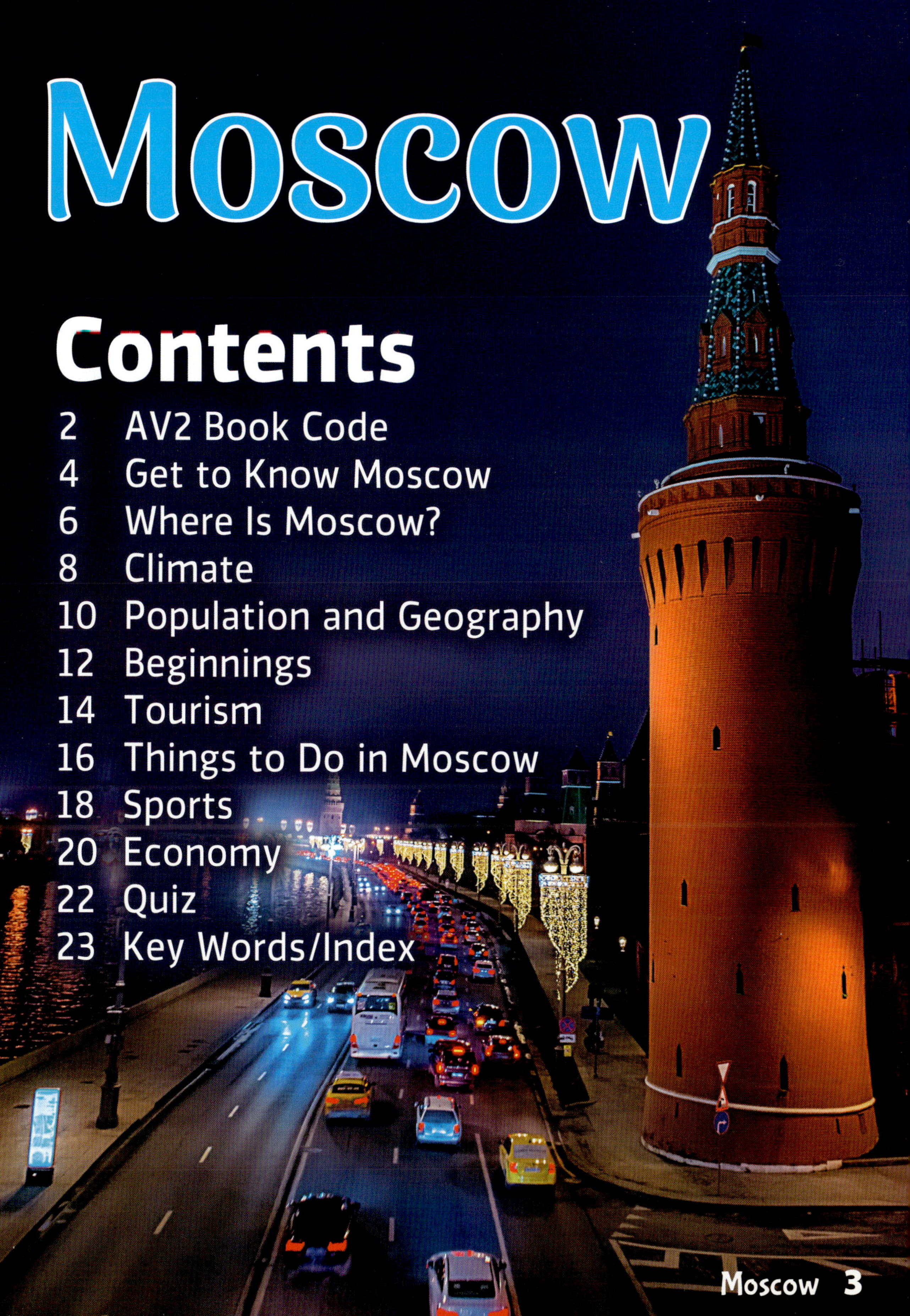

Contents

Get to Know Moscow

Moscow is the capital city of a country called Russia. The city has many unique buildings. Saint Basil's **Cathedral** is known for its colorful domes.

10 Domes for 10 Churches

St. Basil's Cathedral holds 10 separate churches. Each has its own dome.

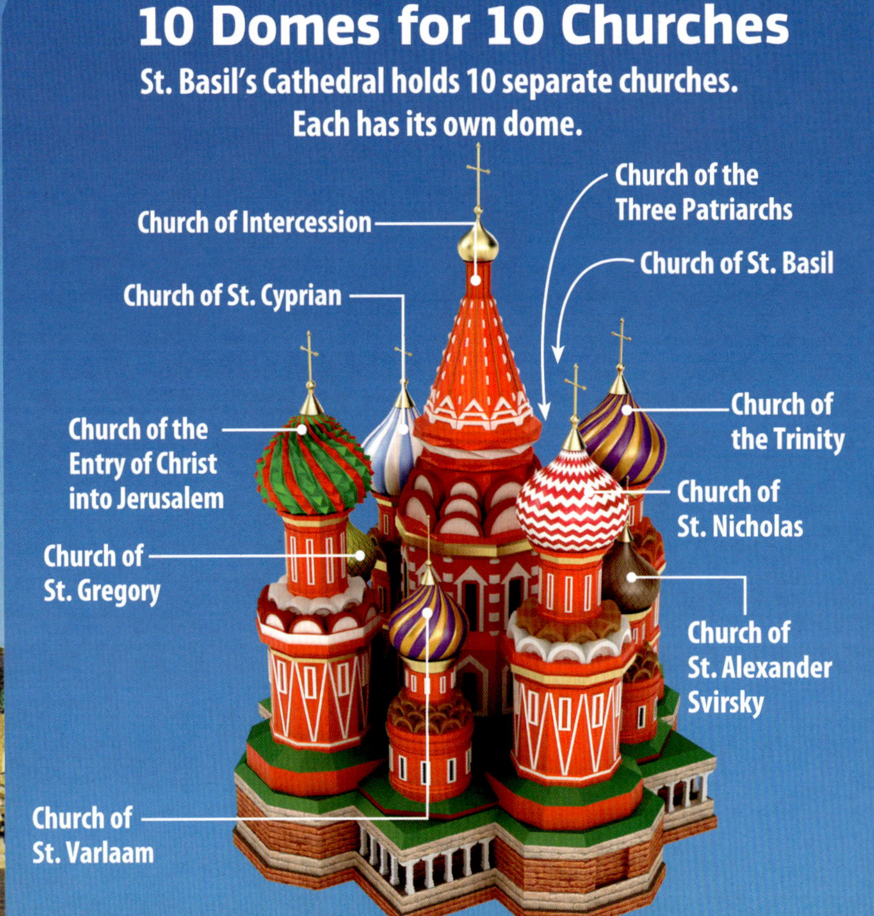

Where Is Moscow?

Arctic Ocean

EUROPE

St. Petersburg is home to palaces, museums, and art galleries.

RUSSIA

MOSCOW

The area around Lake Baikal is a popular place to hike.

Vladivostok is the easternmost point of the Trans-Siberian Railway.

Black Sea

The Caucasus Mountains offer visitors world-class ski hills.

Caspian Sea

ASIA

Pacific Ocean

MAP LEGEND

- Moscow
- Russia
- Land
- Water
- Country border

SCALE

Moscow sits on the western side of Russia. This country is spread across two **continents**. Most of Russia is in Asia. Moscow is in the part that belongs to Europe.

Russia is a large country with plenty to see. Many people visit Russia to learn about its history. Others head to its mountains to ski and hike. Some come to ride a train from one end of the country to the other.

Words to Know

Many people living in Russia speak Russian. See if you can say a few words in this language.

Privet
Hello

Spasibo
Thank you

Do svidaniya
Goodbye

Nyet
No

Pozhaluysta
Please

Da
Yes

Climate

Moscow's **climate** changes greatly from one season to the next. Its summers are mostly warm with a few hot spells. Thunderstorms are common.

Winters in the city can be very cold. They may also be very long. Snow can fall in the city as early as September. It sometimes stays on the ground until April.

A Year in Moscow

Average Summer Temperature
73° Fahrenheit (23° Celsius)

Average Winter Temperature
26° Fahrenheit (–3° C)

Average Annual Rainfall
27 inches (686 millimeters)

Population and Geography

Moscow is Russia's largest city. More than 12 million people live there. Another 8 million people live in the area around it.

The Moskva River runs through the middle of Moscow. The city has 49 bridges crossing this river. These bridges connect the two sides of the city.

Beginnings

Moscow began as a small village thousands of years ago. In 1156, a fort was built to protect the people living there. This fort was called the Kremlin.

Soon, more people moved to the area. Moscow grew into a city. By 1500, it had become a center for Russian **religion** and **government**. In 1918, it was named the country's **permanent** capital.

Moscow Timeline

Many events have taken place in Moscow over time. They helped shape the city into what it is today.

7,000 years ago

A settlement is built in the Moscow area.

1156 AD

A wooden fort called the Kremlin is built at Moscow.

1475

Under the order of Russia's ruler, Ivan III, a rebuilding of the Kremlin begins. This includes the addition of brick walls around the fort.

1712

Another ruler, Peter I, moves the capital from Moscow to St. Petersburg.

1918

Moscow becomes Russia's permanent capital.

2020

Moscow has its warmest winter on record.

Tourism

Today, the Kremlin is one of Moscow's top tourist sites. Inside its walls are palaces, churches, and museums. It is also home to one of the world's largest cannons.

Just outside the Kremlin is the Red Square. It is considered the heart of the city. Important ceremonies and events have been held here for centuries.

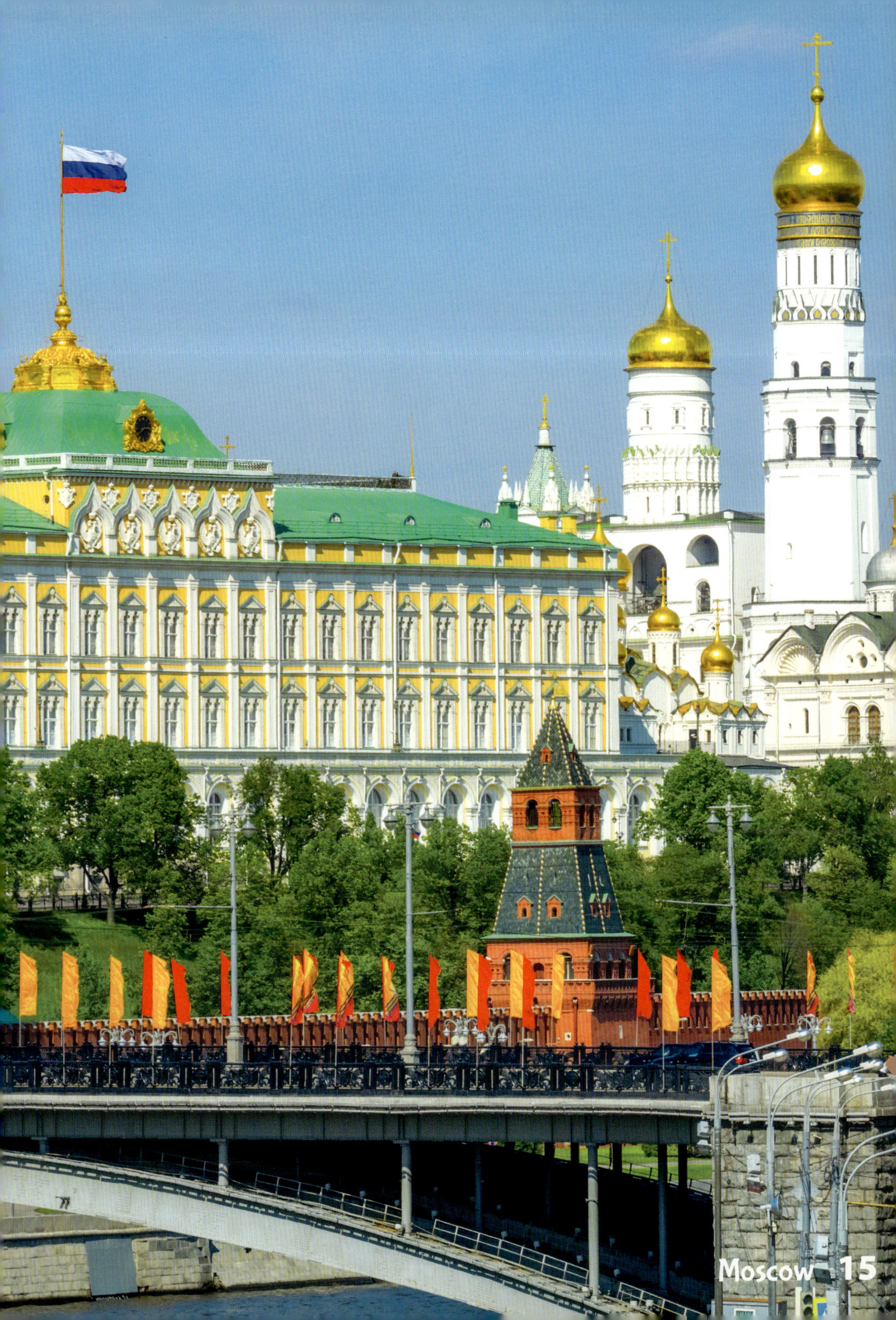

Things to Do in Moscow

Ostankino Tower
Standing at 1,772 feet (540 meters), this tower is the highest structure in Europe. It has an **observation deck** with a glass floor and a **revolving** restaurant.

Moscow Aquarium
This is one of Europe's largest aquariums. Its 80 tanks are filled with more than 12,000 **aquatic** animals.

Gorky Park

As one of Moscow's biggest parks, Gorky Park is a hub of activity. People gather there for dance parties, yoga lessons, and outdoor movies.

Museum of Cosmonautics

This museum explores Russia's history in the field of space exploration. Visitors can see early spacesuits and models of rockets and spaceships.

Bolshoi Theatre

People come from all over the world to watch the many ballets and operas performed at the Bolshoi. This theater has been the **cultural** center of Russia for more than 150 years.

СПОРТ
СОГАЗ
21
88
CCM
ЦСКА

Sports

Soccer is Moscow's main **spectator sport**. Several soccer teams are based in the city. Two of the biggest are CSKA Moscow and Spartak Moscow.

Hockey is Moscow's main winter sport. Its top **professional** team is HC CSKA Moscow. This team plays out of the CSKA Arena. The arena's main ice rink can seat up to 12,000 people.

Economy

People from all over Russia buy goods in Moscow. The city has several large department stores and many smaller shops. They are often crowded with customers.

Moscow is also a center for **manufacturing**. Many **products** are made in the city. They range from cars to animal food.

Moscow's Top 5 Industries

1.  Wholesale and Retail Trade
2.  Manufacturing
3. 

Real Estate
4.  Professional, Scientific, and Technical Activities
5.  Transportation

BLACKGLAMA
Гастроном №1

Quiz

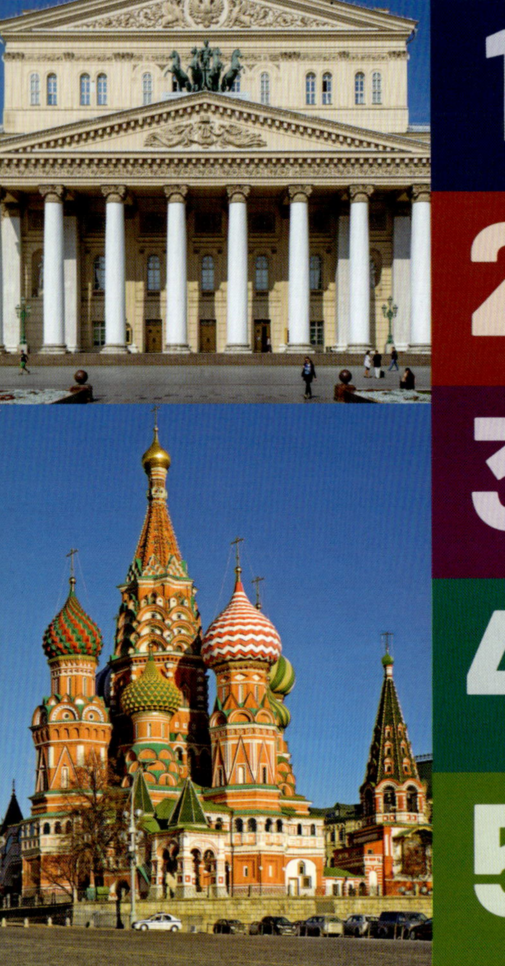

1 Moscow is the capital city of which country?

ANSWER: Russia

2 Is Moscow in Europe or Asia?

ANSWER: Europe

3 How many people live in Moscow?

ANSWER: More than 12 million

4 When was the Kremlin first built?

ANSWER: 1156 AD

5 Which landmark is considered the heart of Moscow?

ANSWER: The Red Square

6 How tall is the Ostankino Tower?

ANSWER: 1,772 feet (540 m)

7 What is Moscow's main winter sport?

ANSWER: Hockey

8 What is Moscow's top industry?

ANSWER: The wholesale and retail trade

Key Words

aquatic: growing or living in the water

cathedral: a large and important church

climate: the average weather conditions of a region throughout a year

continents: the seven main land areas on Earth

cultural: relating to an appreciation of the arts

government: the group of people in charge of managing a country, state, or city

manufacturing: making something, usually with the use of machinery

observation deck: a room or platform that provides views of the surrounding area

permanent: lasting or meant to last

products: things that are made or created

professional: making money by doing something other people do for fun

religion: a system of belief and worship

revolving: moving in a circle around a center point

spectator sport: a sport that people go to watch

Index

Get the best of both worlds.

AV2 bridges the gap between print and digital.

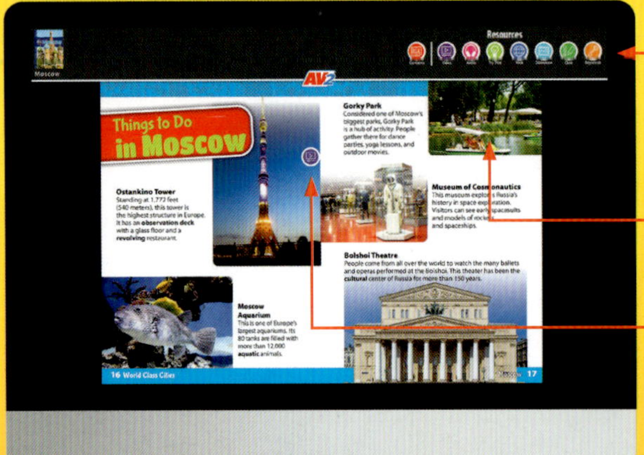

The expandable resources toolbar enables quick access to content including **videos**, **audio**, **activities**, **weblinks**, **slideshows**, **quizzes**, and **key words**.

Animated videos make static images come alive.

Resource icons on each page help readers to further **explore key concepts**.

Published by AV2
276 5th Avenue, Suite 704 #917
New York, NY 10001
Website: www.av2books.com

Library of Congress Cataloging-in-Publication Data
Names: Kissock, Heather, author.
Title: Moscow / Heather Kissock.
Description: New York : AV2, [2022] | Series: World class cities | Includes index. | Audience: Ages 8-11 | Audience: Grades 2-3
Identifiers: LCCN 2021003433 (print) | LCCN 2021003434 (ebook) | ISBN 9781791138363 (library binding) | ISBN 9781791138370 (paperback) | ISBN 9781791138387
Subjects: LCSH: Moscow (Russia)--Description and travel--Juvenile literature. | Moscow (Russia)--Social life and customs--Juvenile literature. | Moscow (Russia)--History--Juvenile literature.
Classification: LCC DK601.2 .K49 2022 (print) | LCC DK601.2 (ebook) | DDC 947/.31--dc23
LC record available at https://lccn.loc.gov/2021003433
LC ebook record available at https://lccn.loc.gov/2021003434

Printed in Guangzhou, China
1 2 3 4 5 6 7 8 9 0 25 24 23 22 21

022021
101120

Project Coordinator: Heather Kissock
Designer: Ana María Vidal

AV2 acknowledges Getty Images, Alamy, and Dreamstime as its primary image suppliers for this title.